# 101 SPOOKY HALLOWEEN JOKES

## by Melvin Berger
## illustrated by Don Orehek

SCHOLASTIC INC.
New York Toronto London Auckland Sydney

ISBN 0-590-47143-0

Copyright © 1993 by Melvin Berger.
Illustrations copyright © 1993 by Scholastic Inc.
All rights reserved. Published by Scholastic Inc.

24 23 22 21                                        16/0

Printed in the U.S.A.                              23

First Scholastic printing, September 1993

*For Benny — the silliest guy I know!*

# GHOSTLY GIGGLES!

The favorite game at the ghost's Halloween party was "Hide and Shriek"!

The young ghost went trick or treating. A neighbor asked her, "Who are your parents?"

"Deady and Mummy," she answered.

The ghost calls home on a terror-phone!

When the boy ghost met the girl ghost,
it was love at first fright!

Where do ghosts go the day before
Halloween?

*To the boo-ty parlor!*

What's the difference between an adult and a ghost?

*One is all grown. The other is all groan!*

One ghost asked another, "Do you believe in people?"

The ghost's favorite days are Moan-day and Fright-day!

What's the difference between a ghost and peanut butter?

*The ghost doesn't stick to the roof of your mouth!*

What do you call a ghost's mistake?

*A boo-boo!*

What's the difference between ghosts and patched jeans?

*Ghosts are dead men. Patched jeans are men-ded!*

**Judy:** What did the daddy ghost say to his son?

**Jody:** Don't spook until spooken to!

The robot turned into a ghost because he couldn't rust in peace!

Where do ghosts go shopping?

*In boo-tiques!*

# WATCH OUT FOR WITCHES!

Why do witches only ride their broomsticks after dark?

*That's the time to go to sweep!*

What did the witch say to the ugly toad?

*"I'd put a curse on you — but somebody beat me to it!"*

How did the witch get around after her broomstick broke?

*She witch-hiked!*

How can you make a witch scratch?

*Take away the W!*

Why do witches ride broomsticks?

*Because they don't have bikes!*

Advice to a witch on a broomstick:
"Don't fly off the handle!"

What is the difference between a witch
and C–A–S–T–S?

*One casts spells. The other spells* casts

**Sam:** Why do witches fly on brooms?
**Pam:** Because vacuum cleaner cords are not long enough!

Some witches are so mean that they plant poison ivy in their gardens!

**Dan:** Why don't witches look into mirrors?

**Jan:** Because it's a shattering experience!

Why is a witch like a candle?

*They are both wick-ed!*

What turns off the lights on Halloween?

*The light's witch!*

What did the young witch say to her mother?

*"May I have the keys to the broom tonight?"*

Why does a witch wear a pointed black hat?

*To keep her head warm!*

# SILLY SCHOOL SPIRIT!

Why are teachers happy on Halloween?

*Because there's lots of school spirit!*

A few days after Halloween, Sally came home with a bad report card. Her mother asked why her grades were so low.

Sally answered, "Because everything is marked down after holidays!"

**Peter:** What subject do witches like best?

**Paula:** Spelling!

On the morning of Halloween, the teacher told the class, "We'll have only half a day of school this morning."

The children cheered.

Then she said, "And we'll have the second half this afternoon."

This time the children moaned!

# PARTY TIME!

Whom did the ghost invite to his party?

*Anyone he could dig up!*

**First Ghost:** Do you need glasses?
**Second Ghost:** No. I'll drink right out
   of the bottle!

Nancy was at Jane's Halloween party. Suddenly it started to rain very hard. Jane asked Nancy if she would like to sleep over. Nancy said yes.

Later Jane saw that Nancy was soaking wet. "What happened?" she asked.

"I went home to get my pajamas!" replied Nancy.

Near the end of her party, Carol said, "Everyone take off your masks."

That made Jack feel bad. He wasn't wearing a mask!

At the class Halloween party, Sandy said to Mandy, "Is this apple cider? It tastes like gasoline."

"No, that's not apple cider," said Mandy. "The apple cider tastes like soap!"

Later Sandy asked Mandy, "Is this Coca-Cola or Pepsi-Cola?"

"Can't you tell the difference?" Mandy asked.

"No, I can't."

"Then what difference does it make?" said Mandy with a shrug.

**Jean:** Everyone was tickled by the fried chicken they served at the Halloween party.

**Dean:** Why?

**Jean:** Because the feathers were still on the chicken!

Two friends at a Halloween party came
dressed as a duck and a cow.

A boy in a King Kong costume
started to chase them. "I want a
quacker and milk!" he said.

# WEIRD MENUS!

What do ghosts eat for breakfast on Halloween?

*Shrouded Wheat.*
*Ghost Toasties.*
*Scream of Wheat.*
*Terri-fried eggs.*
*Rice Creepies.*

What do witches dine on at Halloween?

*Spook-etti.*
*Halloweenies.*
*Devil's food cake.*
*Boo-berry pie.*

When is it bad luck to meet a cat?

*When you're a mouse!*

# BLACK CAT CAPERS!

What happens when a black cat eats a lemon?

*It becomes a sour puss!*

I'm so unlucky that when a black cat
crosses my path, the cat has bad luck'

**Father:** Stop pulling the cat's tail.
**Son:** I'm not pulling. I'm just holding.
The cat is pulling!

How can you tell if a black cat is male or female?

*Ask it a question. If he answers, it's male. If she answers, it's female.*

**Sammy:** What did one black cat say to the other?

**Tammy:** Nothing. Cats can't speak!

What did the black cat do when its tail was cut off?

*It went to a re-tail store!*

# KNOCK-KNOCK NONSENSE!

Knock, knock.
Who's there?
Bea.
Bea who?
Bea-ware, tonight is Halloween!

Knock, knock.
Who's there?
Manuel.
Manuel who?
Manuel be sorry if you don't give me a
   treat!

Knock, knock.
Who's there?
Annie.
Annie who?
Annie body home?

Knock, knock.
Who's there?
Fred.
Fred who?
I'm Fred of witches!

Knock, knock.
Who's there?
Emma.
Emma who?
Emma 'fraid of ghosts, too!

Knock, knock.
Who's there?
Howl.
Howl who?
Howl I know you're not a ghost?

Knock, knock.
Who's there?
Wayne.
Wayne who?
Wayne can I eat my Halloween candy?

Knock, knock.
Who's there?
Philip.
Philip who?
Philip my bag with candy!

# VAMPIRE MADNESS!

**Max:** Do you like the vampire?
**Jake:** Yes, it was love at first bite!

Why do vampires drink blood?

*Soda pop makes them burp!*

Vampires like to play baseball because
they've got plenty of bats!

We could not play kissing games at the party. Three kids came dressed as vampires!

After the party, the vampire sent a fang-you note!

# SCARY SKELETONS!

A skeleton went around breaking
windows on Halloween.

"Aren't you afraid of the police?"
someone asked.

"No. They can't pin anything on me!"

Why didn't the skeleton go trick or treating?

*It had no body to go with!*

He's so skinny that he has to put on
weight to look like a skeleton!

Skeletons that don't work are lazy bones!

A skeleton crew made the witch's broomstick!

Why don't you ever see skeletons fighting?

*They don't have the guts!*

Skeletons get their mail by Bony Express!

The skeleton's favorite musical instrument is the trom-bone!

# COSTUME CAPERS!

Poor Sally! She wore a mouse costume,
and the cat ate her!

One kid wore a sheet over his head.
  "Are you a ghost?" Patty asked.
  "No. I'm an unmade bed!"

Another kid wore a sheet over his head.
  "Are you an unmade bed?" Patty
asked.
  "No. I'm an undercover agent!"

He's so ugly that he poses for
Halloween masks!

My sister dressed as a spoon. When she left the party no one moved. They could not stir without her!

He's so fat . . .
- that he painted himself blue and came as a mailbox!
- that he wore a gray suit and came as a battleship!
- that he painted his belly orange and came as a pumpkin!

He's so dumb that he wore a zebra
costume and said his name was Spot!

She's so fat and her legs are so skinny
that she came as a lollipop!

Bill got the prize for the best costume at the Halloween party. And he just came to pick up his kid sister!

She's so skinny . . .
- that she put on a fuzzy white hat and fuzzy white slippers, and came as a Q-Tip!
- that she took a drink of tomato juice and came as a thermometer!

# TRICK-OR-TREAT LAFFS!

**Kid:** Thanks for the candy.
**Neighbor:** Oh, it's nothing.
**Kid:** I know. But my mother said I had
to say thank you.

Johnny collected nearly two dollars from trick or treating. He went to the store to buy some candy.

"You should give that money to charity," the store owner said.

Johnny thought for a minute. "No, I'll buy the candy," he finally said. "*You* give the money to charity!"

**Kid:** Trick or treat.

**Neighbor:** Here's some candy for you. And here's some candy for your brother.

**Kid:** It's OK. You can have him without the candy!

Jim knocked on the door of a doctor's house. A nurse opened the door. Before he could say anything, she asked, "Do you want to see the doctor?"

"Yes," said Jim.

"Alright," the nurse said. "Come in here and get undressed."

After Jim had taken off his clothes, the doctor came in. "What's wrong?" he asked.

"Nothing is wrong," said Jim. "I just came here for trick or treat!"

**Fred:** Why did the ghost go trick or treating on the top floor?

**Ted:** He was in high spirits!

**Tom:** Trick or treat.

**Neighbor:** Here's an apple if you can spell it.

**Tom:** I–T!

**Tim:** Trick or treat.

**Neighbor:** Here's a banana if you can spell it.

**Tim:** I can spell banana. I just don't know when to stop!

**Jill:** The egg I threw at Mrs. Brown's house is a coward.

**Phil:** How do you know?

**Jill:** Because I saw the egg hit and run.

Why did the boy carry a clock and a
bird on Halloween?

*It was for "tick or tweet"!*

# APPLE TIME!

Marv is so dumb that he carves a face on an apple and goes bobbing for pumpkins!

Al got the most apples when we went bobbing. He wore a snorkel!

Eve also got a lot of apples. She had a mouthful of chewing gum!

Why don't the apples smile when you go bobbing?

*Because they're crab apples!*

# PUMPKIN RIOT!

The one-eyed jack-o'-lantern wore a pumpkin patch over its bad eye!

**City Slicker:** How was the pumpkin crop this year?

**Farmer:** Not too good. Some were as large as potatoes. And they were the big ones!

There once was a man from Brazil,
Who of pumpkin ate more than his fill.
He thought it no matter,
That he grew fatter,
But he burst — which makes me quite
ill!

A farmer from Texas came north to visit a farmer in New York. When they came to the pumpkin patch, the Texan said, "My pumpkins are much bigger than yours."

The New Yorker decided to get even. "Those aren't pumpkins," he said. "Those are oranges!"

What is the difference between a broomstick and a pumpkin?

*You can't make broomstick pie!*

**Tillie:** I wish I had the money for a million pumpkins.

**Millie:** What would you do with a million pumpkins?

**Tillie:** Nothing. I'd just like to have the money!

A fat jack-o'-lantern is a plumpkin!